Shen Jie

ACKNOWLEDGMENTS

When I learn more about eBooks, I try to purchase and download to my device, but I facing that some of the titles are not available in my region.

Therefore, I try many ways to overcome this problem, at last I manage found

a way to download my desire books to my devices-my Pc and my mobile too.

Before you read my information here, please remember that.

This book is for personal use only.

It should serve as a reference only with no guarantee to any personal

and financial gains.

Results from usage of these materials described in this book may vary.

By reading this material, you agree that I not liable on any consequences arising from the usage of this book.

CONTENTS

Acknowledgments

1. WHY AMAZON

Do you know about Amazon .com - a great big shopping site that hosts zillions of products?

They have almost everything that is available to humankind in their online store.

If you enjoy buying online and if you cannot find stuff elsewhere, try looking for your product on their website, and you likely find your product there.

Amazon has these international main sites (Australia, Brazil, Canada, China, France, Germany, India, Italy, Japan, Mexico, Spain, United Kingdom, and Amazon.com-USA)

Buying items from the nearest site to you not always means you to get the items ship to or allow you to download in your individual region.

"Due to copyright restrictions, certain books or eBooks titles are not available in your region."

The information here will guide you how to use a simple tool to enable you to purchase or download the items especially books and eBooks from Amazon , with a simple set up, you actually can buy or download your preferred items and at the best of offered price.

2 .WHY TITLES NOT AVAILABLE

For Amazon.com, most books, DVDs, music and VHS can be ship to almost all destinations outside US.

However, you will be notifying while placing your order they are unable to ship specific items to the address you.

Buyers outside the U.S. cannot purchase the following types of items from sellers: video games, toy and baby items, electronics, cameras and photo items, tools and hardware, kitchenware and house wares, sporting goods and outdoor equipment, software,

In addition, computers, due to warranty issues and manufacturer restrictions prevent them from shipping certain products to all geographical locations.

For books lover sometimes the titles you search appeared this

"Due to copyright restrictions, the titles are not available in your region."

Especially when you wanted to download eBooks from or kindle store, this because some books sold in the Kindle Store have enhanced features, such as X-Ray or Text-to-Speech.

These enhanced features may not be available on all Kindle devices or Kindle reading apps.

When you understand this, you feel despair, but worry no more with the information here.

3 .MANAGE THE SHIPPING ADDRESS

Most of us when open any account in the website, we will fill in our local address for shipping matter, so that the goods will deliver to us correctly.

In Amazon.com if you want to buy books or eBooks when Tittles is not available in your region, you need to add additional Setting in your account, address or shipping address in order for you to buy the products which is fall into restrict category.

"Due to copyright restrictions, certain books or the titles are not available in your region you located."

It means your local shipping address prevent you to shop or buy the item you looking for.

Here is the suggestion, whether you want to buy books, download eBooks or physical products, you need to have the shipping address which is not in their restrict category.

To get the address is simple:

Option 1-

> - go to comgateway.com to get your free US address. With your free U.S. address, you will enjoy the exact same prices, deals, and shipping costs anyone living in the U.S. enjoy too.
>
> For more detail just go comgateway.com and get your free registration.

Option 2-

Visit borderlinx.com –shopping unleashed.

Borderlinx provides package forwarding and international shipping services to ship to you from the US and the UK.

For more detail just go borderlinx.com and get your free registration.

After you obtain the new address, go to
-Amazon.com – your account
-Setting-address book
You're Account > Manage Addresses and 1-Click Settings

ENTER YOUR NEW ADDRESS

Here you add your free US address you get from   comgateway.com   or borderlinx.com.

Now you have two different addresses in your account.

One is your local address and the US address you just fill up.

Next, how to use these two addresses you have in your Amazon.com.

Before you make use of your US address, the application you need to have is Kindle for Pc, Kindle cloud reader, the mobile devices, moreover.

4 .KINDLE FREE READING APPS

"Read more than 1 million* Kindle books on your PC with our free Kindle reading app. No Kindle device required.

Download one of the free Kindle apps to start reading Kindle book in your smart phone, tablet and computer.

You can read thousands of free books with a Kindle reading app, including popular classics like the Adventures of Sherlock Holmes, Pride and Prejudice, and Treasure Island and many more...

The setting is simple:

In your Amazon account: go to
-free reading apps; choose one of the listing devices.
- select your device from listing and download.

-Kindle Cloud Reader,
-Smartphone,
-I Phone, & iPod Touch
-Android, Samsung, Windows Phone, BlackBerry

Computers
- Mac,
-Windows 8,
-Windows 7, XP & Vista,
-kcp_win7_and_before

Tablets
-I Pad
-Android Tablet
-Samsung,
-Windows 8

Choose and select to download to your Android phone or   tablet, I Pad, I Phone, Mac, Windows 8 PC or tablet, BlackBerry, and Windows Phone.

With these free Kindle reading apps, you can buy a Kindle book once, and read it on any device with the Kindle app installed.

In addition, of course, you can read that same Kindle book on a Kindle device if you own one.

With Amazon's Whispersync technology, you can automatically save and synchronize your furthest page read, bookmarks, notes, and highlights across all your devices.

You can start reading a book on one device, and pick up where you left off on another device.

Go into your local library to check out an eBook, and have it delivered wirelessly to your Kindle app.

Your need to have a smart phone may need additional setting each times you about to download items.

5. KINDLE CLOUD READER

Shop for Kindle books directly from Kindle Cloud Reader and download Kindle titles to your device.

From a web browser, visit Kindle Cloud Reader, and then select Kindle Store.

Once completed the download, register with your Amazon account.

Browse for Kindle titles you want to read and then click or tap on a title to view the page detail.

Buy the Kindle title and send it to Kindle Cloud Reader:

From the Deliver to:
On Drop-down menu, select Kindle Cloud Reader.

Note: If you do not see Kindle Cloud Reader in the menu, make sure you signed in with the Amazon account registered to your Kindle Cloud Reader.

Enable Buy Now with 1-Click setting.

6. KINDLE FOR PC

Download and install the Kindle for PC

From your Windows personal computer, visit Kindle for PC
Click Download now, and then follow the on-screen instructions to
download Kindle for PC.

After you finish installing the Kindle for PC app, register the app
with your Amazon account.

About the Version:

The latest version of the Kindle for PC reading app is compatible
with the following devices.

The Kindle for PC app can be use on any computer running
Windows XP, Windows Vista, Windows 7, or Windows 8 or 8.1 in
Desktop Mode.

Note:
Windows 8 RT devices (ARM-based devices) are not compatible.

Register the free Kindle reading app to read

Your Windows computer must be connects to the internet in order to download Kindle content to kindle for PC.

Visit the Kindle Store:

From your computer, click Start, select Kindle for PC app, and then click Shop in Kindle Store.

From Shop in Kindle Store, type your search terms, and then click the search image of search icon.

Sign in to the Kindle Store with the Amazon account linked with your Kindle app.

If applicable, browse for Kindle titles you want to read, and then click on title and view the page.

Buy and send the Kindle title to your Kindle for PC app:

Click the Deliver to drop-down menu, and then select Kindle for PC.

Note: If you do not see Kindle for PC, make sure you signed in with your Amazon accounts.

To buy a book, click Buy Now with 1-Click.

Tip: Click Try a Sample to download the beginning of the book free. After you purchase your content, your titles are delivering to the Kindle app on your Windows computer.

Register your Windows computer.

To register, make sure your Windows personal computer is
connects to the Internet and you have downloaded and installed the
Kindle for PC app.

From Kindle for PC, click Tools, and then click Options.

From the left navigation, click Registration, and then click the register
button.

Enter your Amazon account e-mail address and password.
Click the Register button. Any Kindle content you own appears
under all Items tab.

You can also buy new Kindle titles from the Kindle Store and
download them to your Kindle app.

Update Your 1-Click Payment Method
Purchase books from the Kindle Store with your Amazon 1-Click
Payment Method.

From your computer, visit Manage Your Content and Devices.
You need to sign in to your Amazon account.

Click Kindle Payment Methods.

Under Your Default 1-Click Payment Method, click Edit, and then
follow the on-screen instructions to update your payment method.

Click Continue to verify your changes.

7. KINDLE FOR MOBILE

Kindle for Windows Phone.

-On your Windows Phone, tap the Marketplace tile.

-Tap the Search icon and enter Kindle.

-Tap the arrow button on the keyboard to begin searching.

-Tap Amazon Kindle to open the application's detail page,
then tap Install.

When your installation is complete, tap the Kindle tile on your
Windows Phone to start using the application.

After you finish installing the Kindle app, you will need to
register the app to your Amazon account.

The Kindle app is optimizing for Windows Phones.

Version 2.0.0.6.
Compatible with Windows Phone 8.
Fix for content rendering issues.

Register Kindle for Windows Phone

To buy and read Kindle books, you will need to register your
Kindle for Windows Phone reading app to your Amazon account.

To register, make sure your device is connects to a wireless or data
network and you have downloaded and installed the Kindle for
Windows Phone reading app.

To learn how to download and install Kindle for Windows Phone,
 go to window stores Download & Install the Latest Version of Kindle
for Windows Phone.

Tap the Amazon Kindle tile on your Windows phone to start using the
application.

Enter your Amazon account e-mail address and password.

Tap Register this Kindle. Any Kindle content/books you want to appear
under Archived items.

Note: To view or change your registration, tap Settings on the Kindle app
Menu screen.

Buy & Download to Your Windows Phone

To buy and download Kindle content, your Windows Phone must be connects to a wireless or data network.

From the Kindle for Windows Phone app Home screen, swipe to Kindle Store, and tap on a book cover or Shop Kindle Store.

Browse for Kindle titles you want to read, and your title. View detail page product.

To buy a book, select Buy Now with 1-Click.

After you purchase content, your titles are delivering to the Kindle app on your device.

Deliver books to Your Kindle Library in the Cloud to your Windows Phone reading app.

To successfully delivery to your Kindle content, the Kindle for Windows Phone app must registered with your Amazon account you use to access in order for you to manage your content and devices.

After you buy a Kindle book, the title is saving to your Kindle Library in the Cloud.

Visit Manage Your Content and Devices on Amazon.

Under Your Kindle Library, select the item you want to deliver.

When you locate the item, select Actions, and choose where to deliver to your destination... (Option-if you have another device)

Select the device or app from the Deliver to my drop-down, then select Deliver.

From the Kindle for Windows Phone app Home Screen, select to view all titles.

Kindle for android phone

To download and install Kindle for Android from your phone:

From your Android phone, visit Kindle for Android.
Tap Download now.

Follow the instructions to download the app to your device.

After installing the Kindle reading app, you will need to register with your Amazon account.

About the Latest Version:

The latest version of Kindle for Android is compatible with Android devices running OS 4.0 or greater.

Important: If your device is running an earlier version of The Android OS, you will have the option of downloading the latest compatible version of Kindle for Android

The latest version (4.4) includes the following features and performance enhancements:

Select additional fonts while reading
-Use the enhanced Table of Contents to search and navigate your book (if available)

-Enable and disable auto-brightness while reading
-Faster book cover loading
-Fixed sensitivity when using the volume buttons to turn pages.

Register Kindle for Android Phone

Register Kindle for Android Phone to your Amazon account to buy and read Kindle content.

Before you register, make sure your Android device is connects to a Wi-Fi or data network.

-On your Android tablet, tap the Amazon Kindle app.
-Tap Start Reading.
-Enter your Amazon account e-mail address and password.
-Tap Sign In.
-Tip: To view or change your registration, tap the Kindle icon

-From Home screen, tap Settings.
Kindle for Android features Single Sign On for easier registration.

If you have multiple Amazon accounts, keep in mind that content is not share cross Amazon accounts.

If you are not seeing your books in Kindle for Android, make sure that you are log into the correct Amazon account.

Update Your 1-Click Payment Method

Update your 1-Click payment method to purchase content from the Kindle Store.

From your computer, visit Manage Your Content and Devices on Amazon website.

From the left navigation section, click Kindle Payment Settings.

Under Your Default 1-Click Payment Method, click Edit.

Follow the onscreen instructions to update your payment method.

Kindle for I Phone, iPod touch and I Pad

Download and install the Kindle reading app on your iPod, I Phone, or iPod touch.

From your device, tap the App Store icon in the search box, type Kindle.

From the search results, tap the Kindle app icon.

Tap the Install button to download and install the Kindle app.

After you finish installing the Kindle app, you will need to register the app to your Amazon account.

About the Latest Version of Kindle for I Pad, I Phone, and iPod touch.

Kindle for iOS 4.2 is optimizing for iOS 7.0

Kindle for iOS 4.2 features Smart Lookup.

Press and hold a word or term to see it in the dictionary, Wikipedia, or X-Ray.

Some books now feature a table of contents in the left panel navigation.

Important: I Pad, I Phone and iPod touch with iOS 6.0 or greater

You can download the latest version of the Kindle reading app.

If your device is running iOS 5.0 and you previously downloaded the Kindle application using the Apple account that is associated with your device, you will have the option of downloading a version of the Kindle application that is compatible with iOS 5.0.

Register Kindle for I Phone, I Pad, and iPod Touch

To register, make sure your device is connects to an internet.

From your device, tap the Kindle app icon.

Enter your Amazon account e-mail address and password.

Tap Sign In.

Your Kindle content appears under the Cloud tab.

Note: To view or change your registration, tap the Settings icon on the app Home screen.

-Update Your 1-Click Payment Method

-You will purchase books, magazines, and newspapers from the Kindle Store with your Amazon 1-Click Payment Method, which is a part of your Amazon account.

From your computer, visit Manage Your Content and Devices on Amazon.

From the left navigation, click Kindle Payment Setting.

Under Your Default 1-Click Payment Method, click edit, then follow the on-screen instructions.

Click Continue to verify your changes.

Kindle for BlackBerry 10

To download and read Kindle books, periodicals and personal documents on your BlackBerry 10 device, you will need to first download and install the Kindle for BlackBerry 10 app.

From your BlackBerry 10 device, tap the BlackBerry World icon.

In the search box, type Kindle. From the search results, tap the kindle app.

Tap the download button to install the Kindle reading app.

When installation is completed, tap the Kindle icon on your device to open the reading app and registered it to your Amazon account.

About the Latest Version
The Kindle for BlackBerry 10 app is optimize for Version 1.0
Can be used on BlackBerry 10 smart phones running 10.0.0 or higher

<u>Register Kindle for BlackBerry 10</u>

To buy and read Kindle content, you will need to register your Kindle app to your Amazon account.

Registering also allows you to read all content you own from your Kindle app and any other Kindle devices.

To register, make sure your device is connects to Wi-Fi or 3G and that you have downloaded and installed the Kindle for BlackBerry 10 app.

From your device, tap the Kindle app icon.

Enter your Amazon account e-mail address and password.

Tap Register. Any Kindle content you own appears under the Archive tab.

You can also buy new Kindle content from the Kindle Store and download it to your Kindle app.

To view or change your registration, sweep down from the top of the screen to bring up the Menu and then select Settings.

Deliver to Kindle for BlackBerry 10

Deliver items from Your Kindle Library in the Cloud to your Kindle for BlackBerry 10 reading app.

The Kindle for BlackBerry 10 reading app must be register to the same Amazon account you use to purchase Kindle content.

When you purchase a Kindle book, magazine, or newspaper, it is also saving to Your Kindle Library in the Cloud and can be send it to your phone.

Visit Manage Your Content and Devices and locate the content you want to deliver to your Kindle reading app.

From the Actions drop-down, select Deliver to my...

From the Deliver to drop-down, select your phone, and then select deliver.

Your book or periodical is delivering automatically to your Kindle reading app.

From the Home screen of your Kindle reading app, tap the On Device tab to view and open the title.

SUMMARY

1. Amazon .com a great big shopping site that hosts zillions of products especially books; you can search any titles here.

2 Not all the books or eBooks titles are available to all region.

3 You are able to buy or download if the titles not available in your region with the simple setting in your account setting by add optional address in your shipping address.

4. There are many free kindle reading apps for you to download and read the books.

5. The free kindle reading apps are cloud reader, kindle for pc, and kindle

for tablet, kindle for smarts phone, kindle reader for Black Berry, and kindle for I Phone, I Pad, I Pod touch, window phone and android phone.

6 in order for you to download or buy the titles which is not available you need to obtain the U S address, each time if you buying is not success, go to your account setting, enable your 1-Click setting in your manage shipping page in your Amazon account.

9. THANK YOU

I take this opportunity to thank you to Amazon.com whom provide such a convenient website allow me to have a chance to browse and bought the zillions selection of books.

For those who had purchase this booklet, hope it benefit you from what had shared here.

You are welcome to give me a feedback so that I will improve from here if there is any part of the information here need is incorrect and need to be correct.

You can shares to any one when or if you feel is necessary which you think may help them from this topic.

Shen Jie

Shen Jie